WESTERN RIDING GAMES & CONTESTS

WESTERN RIDING GAMES & CONTESTS

By

BOB GRAY

Editor

THE TEXAS AND SOUTHWESTERN HORSEMAN

Magazine

Cordovan Corporation 1961

Cypress, Texas

The Cordovan Corporation
Cypress, Texas

Western Riding Games and Contests

COPYRIGHT (c) 1961

by

The Cordovan Corporation

SECOND EDITION
PRINTED MAY, 1964
Library of Congress catalogue card No. 61-18122
Printed in the United States of America

CONTENTS

Chapter 1   CALF ROPING   5

Chapter 2   CUTTING   13

Chapter 3   THE BARREL RACE   19

Chapter 4   PRAIRIE STUMP RACE   25

Chapter 5   THE REINING CONTEST   29

Chapter 6   POLE BENDING   33

Chapter 7   THE STAKE RACE   37

Chapter 8   THE FLAG RACE   39

Chapter 9   THE RING RACE   43

Chapter 10   THE BATON RELAY   49

Chapter 11   THE RESCUE RACE   53

Chapter 12   THE POTATO RACE   57

Chapter 13   THE WAGON RACE   61

Chapter 14   THE KEYHOLE RACE   67

INTRODUCTION

Owning a horse is a highly personal, even an emotional thing, so close can you feel to the animal. Many people consider their horses as members of the family, much moreso even than their dogs or cats. It is still common for western stock horses—particularly Quarter Horses—to bear the names of friends or members of the owner's family. Witness such names as Joe Moore, Della Moore, Peter McCue, Joe Reed, Sonny Sykes, Ed Echols—all famous horses past or present.

This closeness to a horse is the stuff of which competition is made. When you own a horse you soon come to feel that this animal is very special. Maybe he isn't the fastest horse alive—but by George, he's got speed! Perhaps he doesn't have muscle in **all** the right places—but then what horse does? True, he **might** be a little long (or short) in the back (or neck) but this sure doesn't hurt his speed or action one bit.

In other words you get proud of that horse—particularly if you just own **one**. And it isn't long before you want others to see what he can do. You soon find yourself wanting to compete, in some way, to demonstrate your horse's ability.

This is not the only reason people like to compete on horseback, of course. Breeders must take their good horses to shows to prove the quality of their bloodline. Most horsemen are filled with a strong competitive spirit themselves and find mounted contests a healthy, exhilarating outlet for their energies. Age doesn't seem to have much to do with this. You'll see people pictured in this book who have been actively retired for years—as well as some still in grade school.

Whatever the motivation and regardless of age, horsemen must have competition—and that's the reason for this book. Stock saddle contests have been spreading across the country with a speed no one can calculate. Nearly all the breeds of good horses have jumped in registrations. Western horse shows have doubled, then tripled in numbers since 1955. Rodeo is growing—and so is the need for more information on how, specifically, the most important western events are being run.

This book doesn't pretend to include **every** stock saddle contest now in use. It covers those which were found to be in widest general use by the most horsemen. Our purpose here is not only to give rules and regulations but to make them **understandable.** Therefore, we have tried to interpret rules and, where possible, to clarify them, so contestants and officials running a contest may enjoy a well-managed event.

Our thanks for cooperation and assistance go to such groups and individuals as the American Quarter Horse Association, George Hatley of the Appaloosa Horse Club, Inc., Teddy Weatherford and the Arlington Saddle Club, members of the Forest Park Saddle Club of Ft. Worth, members of the American Association of Sheriffs Posse and Riding Clubs, the Girls Rodeo Association and Rodeo Cowboys Association. Those wishing the rule books and other information from the major stock saddle organizations may find the following list helpful.

Rodeo Cowboys' Assn., Inc.
320 Boston Building
Denver, Colorado

American Quarter Horse Assn.
P. O. Box 9105
Amarillo, Texas

Girls Rodeo Assn.
Rt 2 Box 122
San Angelo, Texas

Appaloosa Horse Club, Inc.
Box 403
Moscow, Idaho

The American Junior
Rodeo Association, Inc.
Box 1166
Abilene, Texas

National Cutting Horse Assn.
P. O. Box 12155
Fort Worth, Texas

American Association of Sheriffs
Posses and Riding Clubs
Box 242, Spur, Texas

Bob Gray
Cypress, Texas

4

1   CALF ROPING

Calf roping may well be considered the "granddaddy" of stock saddle contests. Roping began with America's ranching industry in the 19th century—and it started through absolute necessity. The first time that a cowboy ever tried to restrain a cow, he found he needed a rope. And the rope and cow pony have since become symbols of the cattle business and the cowboy legend.

Roping today is probably popular among more people than ever before. Mechanization on ranches has reduced the need for roping livestock, but there are many U. S. ranches where the rope is still a basic necessity—particularly in those rugged areas where the horse will always be used for fence repair and cattle roundup. However, the big popularity of roping as a sport is among the non-cowboy contestants, riders who rope for the fun of it—or the profit.

At any small rodeo, you will find that the ropers outnumber nearly all other contestants. Although the luck factor does enter into roping, it's believed that roping takes more training, more practice and more horse-rider coordination than other rodeo events. At least the ropers feel this is true. Certainly, the earning power of a good roper—and his trained horse—is high. "Finished" roping horses—with great speed, stopping ability and intelligence —are worth many thousands of dollars. Top ropers spend years

training such a horse.

Those initials stand for Rodeo Cowboys Association, the group that organized and now regulates professional rodeo at the top earning level. There are also a number of regional rodeo associations and countless rodeo clubs. Many colleges and high schools encourage such groups and they are active within the framework of national organizations like the National Intercollegiate Rodeo Association and The American Junior Rodeo Association. Adding strength to roping as a sport are hundreds of roping clubs in all states. They usually meet from one to four times a month, many have their own arenas and calves. They are filled with people from all walks of life, including doctors, lawyers, bankers and merchants of every type. Roping seems to know no age limits. Some tiny boys rope calves off Shetland ponies as big as their mounts. In Encinal, Texas, every spring there is an Old Man's Roping for men 50 years and over. Roping is a contest that enslaves its enthusiasts, young and old alike!

The Contest

Since tiedown calf roping is the most widely-known phase of the sport, let's consider how the contest is run. Generally, it is held in an arena, more than 200 feet long. The mounted roper starts from a box, chute or alleyway that opens into the arena. A string or "barrier" is stretched across that opening. Alongside the roping box is the calf chute. It too opens into the arena. The roper rides into the box, turns and, when ready, signals for the

Roping, as practiced on many western cattle ranches, often utilizes the old time snubbing post. (left) This is a simple, effective means of restraining an animal for close inspection or medical treatment. One outgrowth of this workaday chore is the south Texas sport of steernecking (below) in which two cowboys team up to restrain an unruly steer.

calf to be turned into the arena. Sometimes, a line will be attached to the calf and secured to the barrier. When the calf has run to the end of the line it automatically jerks the barrier down and that signals the roper to leave the box in pursuit of the calf. That head start given the calf is called the "score." Every rodeo sets its own score, depending on the arena length and other factors. Another way to set the score is by a line marked in front of the calf chute, visible to the roper. He gauges when the calf passes the line and then breaks the barrier with his horse. If there is **no score, or head start for the calf, the contest is called** "lap and tap"—meaning the roper can leave the box at the same time the calf leaves the chute.

Good ropers make the business of catching and tying the calf look relatively easy. It isn't. Several things happen at once. The horse must "rate" the calf quickly and get in position to give the roper a good throwing opportunity. As the rope settles over the calf's head, the roper pulls back the slack to tighten the noose. As the roper shifts his weight to dismount—or gives some other signal—the horse starts a quick, sliding stop. The roper runs down along the rope to the calf, puts the calf on its side and ties any three feet. A flag man in the arena signals the timers, who have kept stop watches on the roper since he broke from the box. Since the score will vary, along with the size and speed of calves, there are no world's records in calf roping.

Rules

In the Introduction to this book, addresses are given so the reader can obtain full, detailed rules of any organization's contests desired, including roping. For our purposes here, a general explanation of calf roping rules will acquaint you with the basic aims of the contest.

"Catch As Catch Can" roping is the name given conventional tiedown calf roping. The roper is permitted to carry two loops, or complete ropes. If he misses with both, he gets no time. The roper is to get no outside help. If his horse drags a calf unnecessarily a roper may be penalized by the flag judge. The roper may tie his rope hard and fast to the saddlehorn or he may "dally" it— that is, take several loops with it—around the horn. In tying the calf, the roper must dismount, go down the rope and throw it to the ground by hand. If the animal is down already the roper must let it stand up, then throw it. Any three feet of the calf must be crossed, then tied with the pigging string. If the tie comes loose or the calf gets to its feet before the judge rules the tie a fair one, the roper gets no time. Flag judges usually allow five seconds from the time the rope horse takes a step forward after roper remounts, to determine whether the tie is secure. The rope should not be removed until the judge has passed on the tie. Arena officials will usually include two or more timekeepers, a tie or field judge, and a deadline or score referee. If the roper leaves the chute before the calf has passed the score line, he is given a 10 second penalty.

Optional Roping

Under this category in amateur roping falls four variations of the contest: Ribbon Roping, Breakaway Roping, Wild Cow Milking and Double Mugging or Team Tying. Goat Roping also is a popular contest in many western youth rodeos. However, in the interest of detailing procedures for the contests in widest use, the first two named events will be covered here.

Ribbon Roping—This contest involves a ribbon being fastened to the calf's tail with a rubber band. The girl member of a two-person team removes the ribbon after her partner has roped and stopped the calf, then runs with it to the judge. The time starts with the roper leaving the box and ends with the girl delivering the ribbon to the judge. The diagram shows the arena arrangement for this event. If the team chooses, both members may be mounted and each may take one loop at the calf. Generally, though, as the contest is most often seen in the southwest, the girl member of the team waits in the contestant's box until her partner has passed the score line, after the calf. If she leaves that circle beforehand, there will be a 10 second penalty. The flag judge shall be in a designated spot on the opposite side of the arena and the girl shall carry the ribbon to him.

The calf must be on its feet when the ribbon is removed. Regardless of who ropes the calf, a girl must get the ribbon

Ribbon Roping Arena Plan

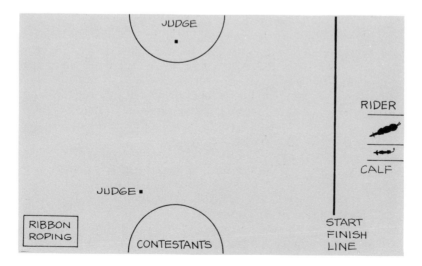

Conventional tiedown calf roping (above and at right) is a test not only of a roper's skill with a lariat but of a horse's training and ability. The good rope horse keeps that line tight as the cowboy puts the calf down and ties three feet. Roper carries pigging string in mouth to free both hands.

from the calf's tail and carry it to the judge. Her partner can hold the calf but cannot help her get the ribbon. If the ribbon slips off before she can get to it, the team is entitled to another calf. Arena conditions will govern the score but from six to 15 feet is considered desirable, by American Junior Rodeo Association rules. Two judges in the field are needed. The flag judge signals time on the ribbon arrival while the other judge, usually mounted, checks the helper's actions in leaving her position and removing the ribbon.

Breakaway Roping—Regular roping rules apply except that the rope must be tied with a string to the horn, or else have a breakaway hondo so that when the calf is roped the loop will be released. The loop must go over the calf's head and the time ends when the string or hondo breaks open to release the loop. Two loops are usually allowed if two loops are carried. This is an ideal contest for young ropers in junior rodeos and youth shows.

Registered Roping

The word "registered" as used here applies to roping contests which are a part of. American Quarter Horse Association performance contests. One primary difference between this roping contest and those already described is that time is not the crucial factor in the Quarter Horse event. A roper has two minutes in the AQHA show to rope his calf and tie it—the horse is judged on how it rates the calf, then assists the roper in completing the

tiedown. That's the point to this event: the horse is being judged in registered roping, not the rider. Here are the rules as drawn by The American Quarter Horse Association:

> **No horse shall be allowed to show in more than one registered calf roping class per show.**
>
> A roping contest will be held under the usual, common rodeo standards and conditions.
>
> Scoring will be done on the basis of 60-80 with 70 denoting an average performance.
>
> Only the performance of the horse is to count. Time of the roper will not count for or against the horse. A time limit of two minutes for each contestant will be allowed.
>
> The roper may throw as many loops in this two minutes as necessary to effectively show his horse. However, if more than one loop is thrown, the roper must carry a second rope tied to saddle and ready. Should roper desire to throw the third, or more loops, he may recoil either rope.
>
> If roper carries only one rope and misses on first loop, he must retire from arena (this provision is necessary to show that horse will work trailing a rope).
>
> The horse will be judged on manners behind the barrier, scoring speed to calf, rating calf, the stop, working the rope and his manners while roper is returning to horse after tie has been made.
>
> Unnecessary spurring, quirting with rope, jerking reins, talking or any noise making, slapping or jerking rope, or any unnecessary action to induce the horse to perform better will be considered a fault and scored accordingly.

2   CUTTING

No other mounted event in the stock saddle field, with the possible exception of calf roping, has developed a body of technique quite as extensive as the cutting contest.

Since 1946, when the National Cutting Horse Association was formed in Ft. Worth, cutting has grown into truly a national sport. In numbers of actual trained cutting horses it is not as large as roping but in terms of the economic value of those horses and the national investment in training facilities, cutting may well rank at the top in the western horse field.

From the spectators' viewpoint, it is a simple form of competition. A rider takes his horse into a herd of cattle, brings one animal out then allows the horse to work with loose reins in keeping the animal from getting back to the herd. Each contestant works two and a half minutes from the time his name is called, and is scored by two judges. The highest score wins.

But appearances are deceiving. This is a highly complex contest, involving such changing factors as the texture of the earth underfoot, proper selection of cattle to cut from the herd, selection of herd holders and turnback men, number of cattle to be cut in one go-round, length of time to work each head, whether the contest is indoors or outdoors—things that can affect the cutting contestant's chances of winning can fill a book, and much has been written on the subject.

To help readers unfamiliar with cutting, some generalizations are in order. For one thing, arena cutting is not like that done

On at least one cow cut from herd, the horse must go "deep"—
to test his ability (above) of moving through herd quietly. The
rider is in control until horse clears herd with his animal. To
score high, horse must work on loose rein. (right) Reining or
cueing counts against horse's score.

on a ranch. Cattle handling often requires cutting herds into small groups, often to pick those animals ready for market. In this case, the cutting horse is expected to move one head at a time from the big herd to the "cut." It is work, not a contest, and the rider doesn't want each cow, steer or calf to do anything but move from one place to another, with no delay.

In the arena, however, turnback men are used to help keep the cut-out animal facing **toward** the competing horse, encouraging competition for the horse. The idea is to give the horse a workout, to let him work with loose reins in keeping the animal from getting past the horse and back to the herd.

Usually the cattle are held in one end of the arena by two herd holders until the contestant has cut out the animal he wants to work. Then the turnback man—often two are used—will prevent the cut-out animal from going any farther up the arena. It's now up to the horse to keep that animal from getting past him. Any help by the rider hurts his chances of scoring high.

The rider can quit that animal anytime he wishes and ride back into the herd for another. When the buzzer or whistle is heard, his time is up. Two judges, usually mounted, are positioned on each side of the arena to score the horses as the rules indicate. They are scoring the horse, not the rider.

Technique

Cutting horses develop their own styles as do human contestants. Therefore, there aren't many hard and fast rules, genuine do's and don'ts of technique, that apply in every case. With judges themselves holding slightly different views, there is variation in how horses will be scored. There is, however, wide agreement on several key points that help determine the outcome of the contest:

Usually the horse that does a good job on two or three head of cattle in his go-round has the better chance to win. Trying to cut more than that doesn't give the horse ample time to really show his ability on any one animal.

On at least one head cut out the horse should go "deep" in the herd and bring the animal back through the herd. Ideally, this would be the first head of stock cut out, if possible.

The horse trained to keep his head low—to look the animal "in the eye"—will show to better advantage to more judges than the high-headed horse.

If the horse begins to "charge" the animal cut out, or in some way "come untrained," it is generally considered better to rein

and correct the horse then and there—and of course be scored low—than to permit the horse to work improperly and risk him continuing to do so later on.

Be ready when your name is called and move instantly toward the herd at that moment. This saves important seconds, allowing you that extra time to show your horse to better advantage.

The Rules

Here are the official judging rules for cutting, as set forth by The National Cutting Horse Association:

1. A horse will be given credit for his ability to enter a herd of cattle and bring one out with very little disturbance to the herd or to the one brought out. If he (or his rider) creates unnecessary disturbance throughout his working period, he will be penalized.
2. When an animal is cut from the herd, it must be taken toward the center of the arena. If it goes down the arena fence, that is all right, but the horse should never get ahead of the animal and duck it back toward the herd to get more play but should let the turnback man turn it back to him.
3. A horse will be penalized 2 points each time the back arena wall is used for turnback purposes; the back fence to be agreed on and designated by the judge or judges before the contest starts; meaning the actual fence only, no imaginary line from point to point to be considered. If any of the contestants voice an objection, before the contest starts, the judge or judges shall take a vote of the contestants, and a "back fence" acceptable to the majority shall be designated and used.
4. If a horse runs into, scatters the herd, lanes or circles the herd against the arena fence, while trying to head an animal, he will be penalized heavily.
5. If a horse turns the wrong way with tail toward animals, he will be disqualified for that go-round with no score.
6. A horse will be penalized 1 point each time he is reined or cued in any manner. If he is reined or cued several times during a performance, he will be penalized each time. When a horse is picked up hard with the reins and set over, or reined, cued excessively, or spurred in the shoulder, a heavier penalty will be marked against him.
7. For riding with a tight rein through a performance, a penalty will be given; for part of the time during a performance, less penalty.
8. If a horse lets an animal that he is working get back in the herd, he will be penalized 5 points.

The trained cutting horse can perform some amazing gyrations in following livestock. This horse, working in ankle-deep mud, has all four feet off ground in following a sudden change of direction by calf.

9. When a horse heads an animal and goes past it to the degree that he loses his working advantage, he will be penalized each time he does so. If a horse goes past as much as his length, he will be assessed a heavier penalty. Unnecessary roughness, such as a horse losing his working position to paw or bite cattle, will be penalized.

10. If a contestant quits an animal he is working when the horse is out of position, or the animal has an undue advantage of the horse, he will be penalized 3 points.

11. A judge marks from 60 to 80 points. An average performance should be marked around 70. A judge should be careful not to mark an average performance too high because the next horse that shows may put on a top performance that deserves 5 or 6 points above average, and if the average performance was marked 75, that would leave no room to give the top horse the credit he deserved above the other.

●

Winning points will be based on a horse's ability to work cattle and the amount of play he gets from the animal during the performance. In other words, if a horse gets good play and shows plenty of ability to cut cattle and the judge thinks he deserves a 78 marking for what he did but he assessed a three-point penalty against him for reining, he would mark him 75.

3 THE BARREL RACE

This event has now become truly a national sport. In every state you can drive through rural areas and see arenas and pastures where three barrels or oil drums stand in a triangular pattern. And that is one reason for the rapid spread and popularity of barrel racing. It takes little more than space to run.

The only equipment needed for the contest is the trio of barrels. They can be secured in most towns and cities for a few dollars from many sources—and this is a contest that an individual rider can practice or run alone.

In spite of barrel racing's apparent simplicity, there are features in the contest which make it a tough one on both horse and rider, particularly from the training standpoint. Not many horses can be of championship caliber because few have both the high speed and the nimble-footed action needed to run hard and fast for a short distance then whip through roughly a 270 degree right turn followed by two left turns almost as sharp.

To teach a horse this kind of control is not easy and many young riders who are eager to win in barrel racing must get experience first. After going to a few rodeos or horse shows they quickly discover the need for a well-bred horse combining the qualities of speed and action. Many horses trained for calf roping make excellent barrel horses although a number of trainers prefer

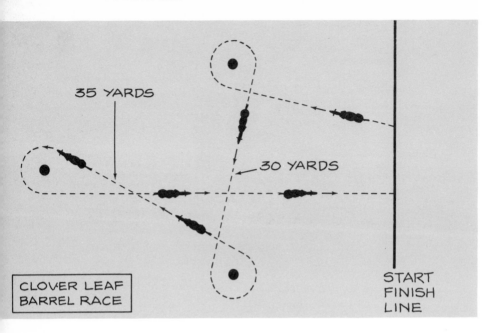

35 YARDS

30 YARDS

CLOVER LEAF
BARREL RACE

START
FINISH
LINE

The Barrel Race Pattern

to start young horses on barrels first and then train for other events later.

The writer recently worked with Jane Mayo, world barrel racing champion, on a book titled "Championship Barrel Racing," which gives much important detail on selection, training and starting a barrel horse. It should be helpful to those seriously interested in professional barrel racing competition.

The Rules

The diagram shows the conventional cloverleaf barrel racing pattern, together with the distances suggested by the Girls Rodeo Association, originators of this contest. It is recommended that the barrels be placed 20 feet from fencelines and that the starting and finishing line be 15 yards from the arena chutes or fences. The standard distance is 30 yards between barrels 1 and 2 and 35 yards between barrels 1 and 3 and between 2 and 3. The first barrel should be at least 20 feet from the starting line. In case an arena is too small to accommodate these distances, the barrels may be closer but not closer than 20 yards apart.

This is a timed event with the contestant starting at a run and being flagged as the nose of the horse crosses the starting line. The nose is also flagged coming back across the finish line.

Knocking over a barrel or not following the pattern set by the rodeo automatically disqualifies the contestant for that go-round

Because barrel racing has become so popular among both contestants and spectators it is now a feature of the largest U.S. rodeos. Trained barrel horses are in much demand and bring high prices.

The speed with which a horse can turn and leave the barrel will often determine whether he will win and place consistently. Longer-strided horses, if properly trained, can have the advantage in this contest.

and the finals. The Quarter Horse rules disqualify a horse if the rider touches a barrel with his hand. The starting line and barrel positions must be marked so that, during the course of the entire rodeo, they will be in the same relative positions for each go-round. relative positions for each go-round.

The contestant has a choice of which barrel—1 or 2—is to be run first. Most contestants will find barrel 1 more desirable to run first since it is the only right hand turn in the race. Barrels 2 and 3 involve left hand turns. It is generally considered easier to run the two left turns in a row, as you do by starting with barrel 1.

Indoor rodeo arenas make barrel racing a year-round sport—but pose a problem for stout horses. Rodeo managements should keep plenty of fill dirt underfoot to give horses a secure base on which to run hard.

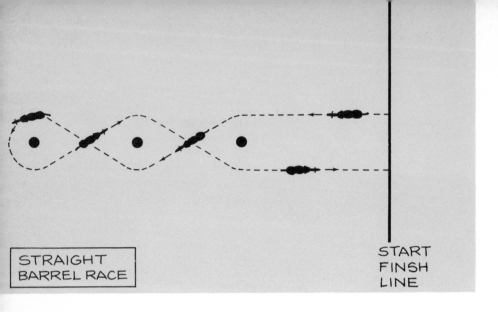

Straight, or Figure 8, Barrel Pattern

Variations

The principal variation in barrel racing is the difference in distances between barrels suggested by the RCA and Quarter Horse competition. The Quarter Horse show rules call for a 25 yard distance from start to barrel 1, then 35 yards between barrels 1 and 2, and 40 yards between 2 and 3 and 1 and 3. Should the arena be too small for this the Quarter Horse shows decrease those distances by five yards at a time. In addition, the horse is disqualified if a barrel is touched by the rider's hand.

Another barrel race pattern still seen in competition is the straight or "Figure Eight" barrel race. Its use as a rodeo contest actually pre-dates the cloverleaf pattern, according to veteran contestants, but did not prove as widely popular as the triangle barrel arrangement.

The contestant goes to either side of the first barrel in the straight pattern, then does a figure eight around the two remaining barrels, as shown. This contest is still used at a number of youth rodeos since it does not put quite the same demand on a horse as the cloverleaf pattern does.

Camas Prairie Stump Race requires most of space in a sizable arena. This shows start of race.

4   CAMAS PRAIRIE STUMP RACE

The Nez Perce Indians of the Pacific Northwest were fanatics on the subject of horse racing. They loved short races—from a starting line to a tree, perhaps, and back again. Frequently riding Appaloosa ponies, the Indian braves would spend many an afternoon racing and betting on favorite horses—and maybe losing a lot of wampum in the process. The matched race—horse against horse—was their sport and this accounts for the modern variations of these early Indian contests.

The Camas Prairie Stump Race is one currently popular among Appaloosa breed enthusiasts. It is a standard performance event at Appaloosa horse shows and got its name from the Indian matched races that often used a stump on the prairie as a turning point.

This is not a timed event. As the diagram shows, it is really a double barrel race, with each of the two mounted contestants running identical cloverleaf barrel patterns. They start from a common starting line at the signal of an official. They finish at the same line, going in opposite directions.

The Start

It is sometimes difficult, as in many matched races, to get both horses off to a "clean" start. The judge or starter usually blows a whistle or drops a flag when it appears that both horses are positioned at equal distances from the starting line. At the judge's discretion horses that get away to a bad start may be called back to start again.

A perfect start would have both horses crossing the line at same instant—and judge in matched race such as this may call horses back several times before getting them off to equal start.

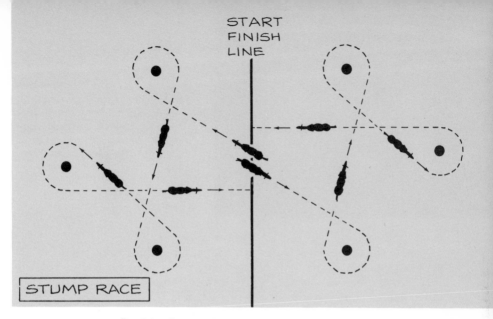

STUMP RACE

Prairie Stump Race Pattern

The Pattern

The two opposed three-barrel courses are set up with a common starting-finish line. The two front barrels are 30 feet from that line and are 75 feet apart. The back barrel is set 94 feet from the finish line, in Appaloosa shows. Running positions are drawn by (or for) the contestants and the Bye system is used in the event of an odd number of entries.

Excitement in a matched race affects contestants as well as the crowd. They can sense who's ahead.

Horse in background takes the lead as he circles the last barrel and heads for the finish line. The eliminations system may require winner to run several heats, to determine show champion.

Eliminations

The horses will race the triangular pattern by starting with the barrel on the contestant's right as he approaches the starting line. The conventional cloverleaf pattern is followed throughout and a horse that knocks over a barrel is eliminated. Also cause for elimination is a contestant turning a barrel the wrong way or touching the barrel with his hand, so as to steady it. If both entries commit similar infractions, the two contestants may run the heat again, until one horse finishes without penalty.

To determine the final winner among a number of horses in this event it is necessary to run several heats. Losers are then paired against losers to determine the 3rd, 4th and lower-placed horses. In larger contests you may need to run winning horses three, four or even five heats before a champion is named. The contest thus becomes a good workout for any horse—and a fine crowd-pleasing event as well.

Horse at left is the winner

First thing a judge sees in the reining contest is the way a horse stops. Hindquarters should be well up under horse and head should be down, as shown.

5 THE REINING CONTEST

This event is a familiar fixture at most western horse shows, whether they are sponsored by a breed association or by a group staging an "open," all-breeds, or youth show. The event, generally, is supposed to determine how well a horse can rein, stop, change leads and be handled smoothly by the rider. One group which has devoted much time to developing the contest is The American Quarter Horse Association.

Because livestock control—particularly the cattle business— calls for a using horse with exceptional reining ability, that breed has emphasized the importance of this contest. It is held at nearly all approved Quarter Horse shows. We have therefore included here the bulk of the AQHA rules governing the reining contest, realizing that various non-Quarter Horse groups may need to adapt them in different ways to particular needs. Those contestants who can successfully run the accompanying reining pattern in the prescribed manner should be well prepared for nearly any variation they may encounter. One of the biggest reasons for riders not doing well in this event is the contestant's inability or failure to follow the pattern. Before reining patterns are run it is customary for the judge to ask a rider to "set the pattern"—that is, go through it one time so that all contestants will know what they're expected to do.

The Rules and Pattern

All contestants concerned will gather at the arena at the proper time. Upon call, each contestant will perform the required pattern individually and separately.

The arena or plot should be approximately 50x150 feet in size.

Each horse will be judged on the neatness, dispatch, ease, calmness and speed with which it performs the pattern. Excessive jawing, open mouth or head raising on stop, lack of smooth sliding stop on haunches, breaking gaits, refusing to change lead, anticipating signals, stumbling or falling, wringing tail, backing sideways, knocking over stakes or kegs, changing hands or reins, or losing stirrup, or holding on, or two hands on reins, or any unnecessary aid given by the rider to the horse (such as unnecessary talking, petting, spurring, quirting, jerking of reins, etc.,) to induce the horse to perform will be considered a fault and scored accordingly. Horse shall rein and handle easily, fluently, effortlessly, and with reasonable speed throughout the pattern.

The figure eights are designed to test horse's ability to stay on right and left leads, as well as change leads. On right lead, right forefoot is extended. Rider has slightly more weight in right stirrup.

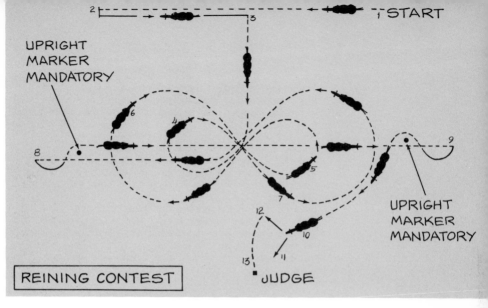

The Reining Pattern (A.Q.H.A.)

PATTERN INSTRUCTIONS

- Run from 1 to 2 at full speed and at least 20 feet away from any existing fence or wall.
- Stop and back.
- Settle horse for 10 seconds.
- 4 & 5, Ride small figure 8 at slow canter.
- 6 & 7, Ride large figure 8, fast.
- Left roll back over hocks. Upright markers are mandatory at points marked X on pattern.
- Right roll back over hocks.
- Stop.
- Pivot left.
- Pivot right.
- Walk to judge and stop for inspection until dismissed.

Failure to follow and execute the pattern as set forth will be considered a fault and scored accordingly.

Scoring will be on the basis of 60-80 with 70 denoting an average performance.

In case of doubt, a judge may require any contestant to repeat his performance of any or all the various parts of the pattern. A judge, also, shall have the authority to require the removal or alteration of any piece of equipment or accoutrement which, in his opinion, would tend to give a horse an unfair advantage. Any inhumane equipment will be scored accordingly.

A (Quarter Horse) show may have up to three approved reining classes. If three reining classes are to be held, they should be the following:

    (a) Senior Reining (five year olds and older, all horses must be shown with a bit.)

    (b) Junior Bit Reining (four year olds and younger, all horses to be shown with bit.)

(c) Hackamore Reining (four year olds and younger, all horses to be shown with hackamore.)

If two reining classes are to be held at a show, they should be the following:

(a) Senior Reining (as specified above).

(b) Junior Reining (four year olds and younger, horses may be shown with either bit or hackamore at the discretion of the exhibitor.)

If only one reining class is to be held at a show, it should be the following:

(a) Reining (all ages—horses five years old and older must be shown in bit; horses four years old and younger may be shown in either bit or hackamore at the discretion of the exhibitor.)

In straight hackamore classes, two hands may be used. In combined bit and hackamore classes, only one hand on reins of bit or hackamore.

FOR HACKAMORE REINING, horses will be ridden ONLY with a rawhide braided or leather braided or rope bosal. Absolutely no iron will be permitted under the jaws regardless of how padded or taped.

For BIT REINING, horses will be ridden with grazing, snaffle, curb, half-breed, bar or spade bit. However, no wire curbs, regardless of how padded or taped, or no chin strap narrower than one-half inch, or no nose bands or tiedowns will be permitted.

Chain curbs are permissible but must be of the standard flat variety with no twist and must meet the approval of the judge.

Horses, five years old and older, must perform in the bit reining class.

A Rider May Ride Only ONE Horse per Reining.

FAULTS AGAINST THE HORSE

1. Opening mouth excessively in Bit Reining.
2. Breaking gaits.
3. Refusing to change leads.
4. Anticipating signals.
5. Stumbling and falling.
6. Wringing tail.
7. Bouncing or sideways stop.
8. Backing sideways.

FAULTS AGAINST THE RIDER

1. Changing hands on reins.
2. Losing stirrup.
3. Two hands on reins at any time.
4. Any unnecessary aid given by the rider to the horse (such as unnecessary talking, petting, spurring, quirting, jerking of reins, etc.) to induce the horse to perform will be considered a fault and scored accordingly.

6   POLE BENDING

For several years pole bending has been increasing rapidly in popularity until today it is, with barrel racing, among the most frequently-run events at horse shows and youth rodeos. It is also the kind of contest that can be staged almost anywhere for nearly any group of horsemen. It appeals to riders of all ages and the event tests the horsemanship of the riders as well as the "action" of his mount.

Pole bending has been adopted as a standard performance event by both The American Quarter Horse Association and The American Association of Sheriffs Posses and Riding Clubs. There are slight variations in the way these two organizations run the race.

The AQHA rules call for six poles to be set 21 feet apart with the first one set 21 feet from the starting line. The AASP & RC rules requires six poles with a 30 foot interval between poles and the first pole 30 feet from the starting line.

The Pattern

Each contestant begins the pole bending race from a running start. Time begins as his horse's muzzle crosses the starting line. The Quarter Horse rules call for two watches to be kept on the race with an average of those times to be the official time for the contestant. A flag man will customarily signal the timers as each contestant starts and finishes.

The rider may go to either right or left of the first pole. He

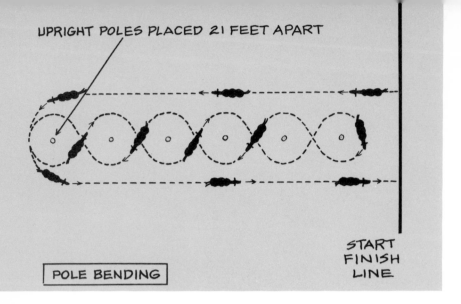

UPRIGHT POLES PLACED 21 FEET APART

POLE BENDING

START
FINISH
LINE

A.Q.H.A. Pole Bending Pattern

then weaves the horse through the line of poles to the last one, turns and weaves back through the poles to the finish line.

Penalties

In the AQHA rules, knocking over a pole, touching a pole with the rider's hand or failing to follow the prescribed pattern causes the contestant's disqualification. The Sheriff's Posse rules penalize a rider 5 points for knocking over or touching a pole to steady it, and disqualification results from failure to weave through all of the poles.

In event of a tie in Quarter Horse pole bending, the horse declared the winner must have run the pattern, in the runoff, within two seconds of the original time or else the runoff shall be held again.

A quick rollback at end of course can save time (below left) and give horse a chance to brace for the stretch drive back through poles. (right)

Observant flag men at the finish line are important to every timed event. Noses of horses should be flagged, starting and finishing, and consistent flagging helps timers do the best possible job.

Equipment

Poles or stakes from five to seven feet long are customarily used in this contest. They can be square or round and can be held upright either by braces on four sides of the bottom or by disc-type bases. The AASP & RC rules call for pole bases no more than 17 inches in diameter with rubber hose covering the edge if discs are used. Maximum weight allowed for the base is 12 pounds.

As for contestants, the choice of bits and bridles is optional in this contest although judges may prohibit the use of any equipment they may consider too severe.

Training and Technique

The best pole bending horses are usually those that rein exceptionally well and have lots of action. Speed is not always the deciding factor in this race since the horse has only a short distance to run at full speed.

Another winning characteristic in pole bending is the rhythm needed for a horse to dodge through the line of uprights, changing leads every few strides. The size of a horse will determine the length of his stride—and a rider should establish how many strides his horse can take between poles before he changes leads. Knowing this, you can help your horse develop an even, smooth run. Pulling the horse sharply to the right or left around each pole will cost much valuable time and reduce the chance of the horse falling into a rhythmical pattern.

The turn or rollback at the last pole is another time-consuming step in the race. The horse with a good stop and rollback may have an edge over the horse that must run in a circle to change direction.

As with all of the race-type contests, pole bending winners aren't necessarily those that run the pattern most often. Rather they are horses whose ability is developed through lots of pasture work, reining practice—and wet saddle blankets. Few of the pole benders will run the pattern at home, once their horses are trained.

7 THE STAKE RACE

As the photographs illustrate, stake racing is essentially the same type race as pole bending, with two important differences. Where pole bending is a timed event in which one horse runs through the poles against a stop watch, stake racing is a matched race between two horses. There is a difference also in the way the pattern is run.

Stake racing is now one of the most popular events at youth shows and open horse shows, as well as among Appaloosa horse owners.

As the Nez Perce Stake Race it is one of the official performance events of the Appaloosa Horse Club, Inc. The rules given here follows that group's established procedures.

Two adjacent six stake courses are set up, with a common starting-finish line. The first stake shall be 20 feet from the starting line and other stakes shall be 21 feet apart.

The Pattern

The two horses, started together, will run along the right hand side of the twin courses to the end stake, circle the stake to the left and weave through the stakes in the direction of the finish line. At the first stake they will reverse to the right, bend back through the stake to the last one, circle to the left and race straight back to the starting line. (see pattern)

It will be apparent from this that the two adjacent lines of stakes must be set far enough apart so that the two horses, particularly in turning, won't interfere with each other.

The Start

The skill of the judge or arena official comes into play in starting any matched race, and the stake race is no exception. The starting official usually will blow a whistle in signaling the

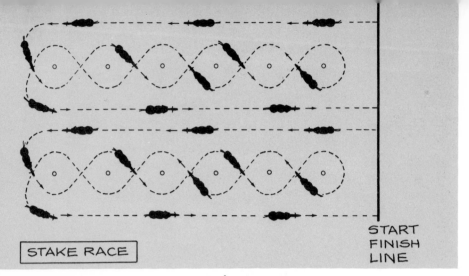

START
FINISH
LINE

Stake Race Pattern

start of the race. The two riders bring their horses to the starting line and when, in the official's opinion, they are equally ready he signals for the start. If, in his opinion, it is not a "clean" start, he may call them back to start again. This is one phase of the race where a rider with his horse under good control can enjoy some advantage. The excited, unmanageable horse is much harder to start properly than the poised, alert animal. And a rider can have a positive effect on a horse's attitude in such races. You may have noticed that the calm, self-controlled contestant often wins the matched race—and that his horse exhibits the same characteristics.

Penalties

Knocking down a stake, turning the wrong way or the rider touching a stake with his hand are the three main causes for stake race disqualification. If, however, the other contestant in the race incurs a similar infraction, the heat can be run again— until one or the other of the horses finishes without penalty.

There are other penalties that can be imposed, of course. Open and youth shows often set up ground rules which levy a two second penalty for touching a pole, to steady it. Knocking over the stake or failing to follow the pattern nearly always means disqualification. Many shows also reserve the right to disqualify a rider for unsportsmanlike conduct.

Eliminations System

Since many shows will have large numbers of stake racers it will be necessary for the winning horses to run the pattern several times to obtain a first place winner. Customarily in the Appaloosa contests positions are drawn for heats, with the bye system being used in the event of an odd number of entries.

Winners are then run against winners until the heat which brings together the two finalists. The loser is the second place winner. Third and fourth places are determined by matching the losers in the semi-final races.

8   THE FLAG RACE

In some parts of the country the flag race has been a contest event as long as—or in some cases longer than—the barrel race. It was one of the forms of competition that became popular among the wives of rodeo cowboys, when the girls got tired of sitting in the stands watching their husbands compete. Soon the ladies were stirring up arena dust themselves.

As it has finally evolved the flag race can be as tough a contest to win as nearly any other. It requires some quick handwork on the part of the flag-carrying rider and some agile footwork by the horse. It's also exciting for spectators to watch.

In brief, this contest finds three flags being used. The rider carries one, two others are in buckets attached to either side of the arena. The contestants rides around by the buckets exchanging flags as fast as he can. It is a timed event.

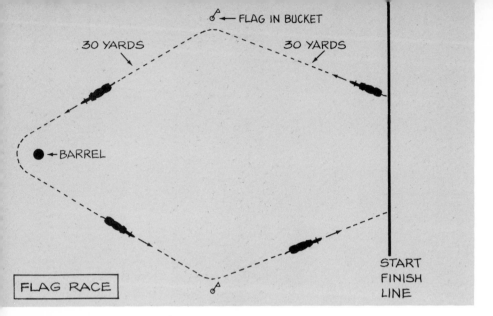

FLAG IN BUCKET

30 YARDS   30 YARDS

←BARREL

FLAG RACE

START
FINISH
LINE

Flag Race Pattern   (A. A. S. P. & R. C.)

Equipment And Rules

The three flags used in the contest are about 6 x 8 inches in size, of different colors and should be on flag sticks about 14 inches long. The two buckets used should be conventional three gallon buckets, filled nearly to the top with sand. They should be placed parallel to each other, one on each side of the arena, and about four feet off the ground. They should be about 30 yards from the starting-finish line.

To complete the pattern a barrel should be placed in the center of the arena and about 30 yards from, and slightly beyond the buckets.

As each contestant enters the arena, he is handed the first flag. His time starts as his horse reaches the starting line. He plants the flag he was given in the first bucket, grabs the flag already there, rides around the barrel to the second bucket, changes flags there, and then rides across the finish line. Time ends as the horse reaches the finish line.

As contestants enter the arena they should be handed the first flag. Their time begins as horse's muzzle reaches starting line. They should hand last flag back to this same official.

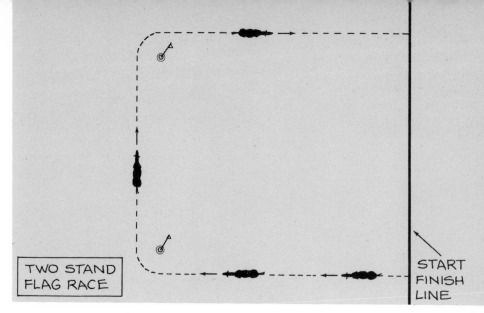

TWO STAND FLAG RACE

START FINISH LINE

Flag Race Pattern (G. R. A.)

Most Girls Rodeo Association contests currently feature the barrel race and the above pattern is not seen as widely as in the past. Flag race rules in this chapter therefore refer to the pattern on the opposite page.

The rider can make the circle from either left to right or right to left. If he drops the flag on the ground he must dismount and retrieve the flag in order to continue the race. He must be mounted as the flag exchanges are made. If the flag falls over, but stays in the bucket, the contestant's time counts. But if it falls out of the bucket and the rider does not replace it, then his time does not count. If wind or weather causes it to fall out the judges will have to rule on whether the time counts. Contestants who use a flag to strike their horses should be disqualified.

Contest Tips

The calm horse with a good stop can help you win this one. Biggest obstacle to a good time in the flag race is the difficulty

Overshooting the barrel means the contestant must return, reach across the horse for the flag change—unless choosing to switch rein hands. This is where race can be won or lost.

Approaching first flag, control is as important as speed. Rider will try to stop only the instant needed to jam in one flag, grab the other and go.

of making a fast, sliding stop exactly in front of the flag bucket—and close enough so that the rider can switch flags in an instant.

Many contestants make the mistake of starting too fast, then overshooting the bucket. By the time they stop, roll back and return to the bucket they're heading the wrong way and must either change rein hands or else reach across with the free hand to make the flag switch. Best bet is to go slower on the first bucket, make a smooth, controlled change, then increase speed to the second bucket. Frequently it isn't the fastest horse that wins the event but the best-controlled horse.

Again, as in all race-type contests, better not practice all day for this one. If you've put a good stop and a good rein on your horse you've got as much chance to win as anybody.

This contestant must now dismount and put the falling flag back in the bucket—if she wants her time to count.

9 THE RING RACE

The ring race is a test not only of a horse's speed but the skill with which horse and rider can work together in a rapidly-run contest.

The object of the event is to see how many rings a rider can spear from horseback while running a circular course in an arena. There are six rings in all, three on each side of the arena. It is a timed event. You spear the rings with a tapered stick of wood approximately 30 inches long, to which is attached a wood or plastic shield about eight inches from the base, or holding end. This catches the rings as they are speared. (A cut-down billard cue makes a good spear.)

As played by member clubs of the American Association of Sheriffs Posses and Riding Clubs, the ring race starts when a horse's nose reaches the starting line. The contestant races down one side of the arena, spearing the rings along the way, circles a barrel at the end of the arena—placed 180 feet from the starting line—then comes down the other side of the arena and spears the other three rings. Time ends when the horse's nose reaches the finish line. One line all the way across the arena serves as both starting and finishing line.

As the contestant enters the arena, an official hands him the spear. After the run he will hand the spear back along with the rings he has been able to snare.

A one-second penalty is added to a contestant's time for each ring that is missed. A rider must spear two rings to qualify. A rider is also disqualified if he uses the spear to hit his horse or if the spear is held farther than eight inches from the base end.

The rings must still be on the contestant's spear or arm when he completes the ride. Riders can circle the pattern in either direction.

A flag man customarily signals when a contestant starts and completes the race. One person is also needed behind each ring support to put another ring in place after it has been speared. To keep the event moving rapidly a man on horseback at the finish line can collect the rings from finishing contestants and redistribute them to the people keeping the rings ready.

Equipment Needed

Rings used in this contest are plastic rings, perferably all of the same color, about five inches in diameter. They are suspended just inside the arena by the use of 2x4 inch overhanging arm which is attached to an upright post along the arena's edge. If ring races are to be run frequently in your arena such an upright post can be set into place when the fence is built, and the arm put on hinges.

The overhanging arm should extend into the arena about 30 inches. Nail a piece of heavy leather or rubber strap that hangs down 12-14 inches from the arm. A clothespin attached to the end of the strap will hold the plastic ring securely until speared by the passing rider.

Close-up of ring and supporting arm. Notice that arm is hinged so it can be swung back out of the way when not in use. Strap should be heavy so wind won't blow ring back and forth.

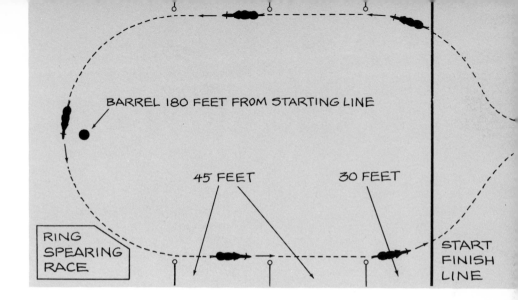

BARREL 180 FEET FROM STARTING LINE

45 FEET

30 FEET

RING
SPEARING
RACE

START
FINISH
LINE

Ring Race Pattern

When completed, these posts and arms should suspend each of the six rings at about shoulder-height to the average man on horseback. It's a good idea to get the overhanging arm above head-height to avoid the chance of an accident. The strap that hangs down should have a buckle in it so that the height of the ring can be adjusted for men, women and children contestants. The heavier a material the strap is made of, the less sway there will be from gusts of wind.

The rings are spaced about 15 yards apart with the 1st and 6th rings placed 30 feet from the starting-finish line.

Risks Involved

Raising the overhanging arms above head level should eliminate a major risk to riding safety in this contest. Another risk involves

Clothes-pin releases ring easily upon being speared. Ring race can be kept moving rapidly if helpers can be positioned behind each ring stand to replace them as needed.

Contestant here is far enough away from ring to avoid hitting head on crossbar—but care should be taken in building ring supports to get them well up away from taller riders' heads.

Contestants who win frequently in this event appear to sight down their arm or spear, keeping it in roughly the same position along both sides of course.

On the fourth ring stand the horse is curving in from barrel and isn't as close to rings as his rider might want—however, that spear can make up a lot of distance!

the way an arena is shaped. Ideally, the race would be run in an arena with two gates at the same end. Then contestants could enter one gate, run straight down the fence line of rings, circle to the other side and ride straight out the other gate. Most arenas, however, will have a single entrance at one or both ends. Thus, on the 6th ring a contestant may be riding at full gallop and experience difficulty in reining away from a fence line, stopping and still retaining control of the spear and rings. This is one reason why experienced contestants will make sure they are in full control as they approach the 6th ring, prepared to pull off toward the alleyway.

Training For The Event

Basically, the training problem here is to teach a horse to run in a straight line at a good rate of speed—and at a fixed distance from a fence or wall. Riders who win in this event consistently start a horse in it by riding easily and slowly by the rings a few times, to establish in the animal's mind how far from the ring he should stay. Some horses will shy away from them. Also it is necessary to keep the horse on a left lead since you will have to rein to the left and circle the barrel, going from the 3rd to the 4th ring. The horse will move more easily and quickly around the barrel if he is on the proper lead. (It is permissable to run the rings from right side to left, if a rider is left handed. Then, of course, the horse should stay on a right lead.)

In a strange arena it is also a good idea to approach the starting line slow. Make certain your horse knows the direction you plan to run and the route. Contestants who ride into an arena on the run, then head for the first ring without allowing the horse to get his bearings are expecting quite a bit from the animal. A slower approach to the starting line will also allow you to run a straighter line at the first three rings.

10   THE BATON RELAY

The Baton Relay may well be considered the most difficult and spectacular contest in the Playday schedules sponsored by The American Association of Sheriffs Posses and Riding Clubs.

It is difficult from the contestants' standpoint because it requires the utmost in teamwork—particularly in the passing of the baton from one rider to another on horses in motion, within a small area. It is spectacular from the spectators' standpoint since the event puts three riders in the arena, running close together, and the chances for mishap are correspondingly greater than in most timed events.

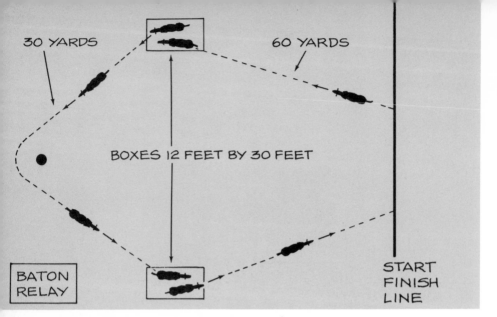

30 YARDS

60 YARDS

BOXES 12 FEET BY 30 FEET

BATON RELAY

START FINISH LINE

Baton Relay Pattern

The diagram shows the pattern to be followed. Each team is composed of three contestants on horseback. One rider, carrying the baton, starts the run from a starting-finish line. A flag man is needed to signal the timers. The event begins with a running start.

The baton is exchanged twice, on opposite sides of the arena. The first rider hands it off to the second rider, who is stationed in a 12 x 30 foot pen along one arena fenceline. The second rider races around the barrel in the center of the arena and hands the baton to the third rider, who is stationed in the other pen. Rider number three then races for the finish line.

Both exchanges must be made within the confines of the pen. It is marked on the ground with either flour or lime and if the exchange takes place outside its boundaries, the team is no-timed. In making the exchange, the oncoming rider may pass on either side of the rider waiting to receive the baton.

If the baton is dropped during the exchange, either rider may dismount, pick it up and continue the race. But if the baton is dropped outside the pen, the contestant who drops it must pick it up.

A good supply of lime or flour is a must so the boxes can be kept clearly outlined on the ground. Judges must be able to see if there is a fair exchange in the box.

As the baton changes hands rider on left will race around barrel and hand it to third rider in other box. First rider on right will rein in after hand-off to avoid danger of collision. Both horses are in motion at time of hand-off.

Equipment And Distances

One barrel, two marked-off pens and the baton are needed to stage this contest. The baton is usually some soft, non-injurious material—such as a length of hose—not over 18 inches long. The pens are marked off 60 yards from the starting-finish line and the barrel is placed in the center of the arena 30 yards from the pens at approximately a 45 degree angle, (See diagram) as the horse will run leaving the first pen.

If a number of teams are going to run this event, it is well to have a good supply of lime or flour on hand to keep the pens freshly marked since this is where many disqualifications take place. The baton exchange can be rapid and the lines need to be clear for judges to determine if it was a fair exchange. In addition, many clubs and shows will use one extra judge at each pen to insure the close supervision of the exchange.

Another violation judges watch for is whether the third rider crosses the finish line with the baton, as he should, before his two teammates. Both riders one and two were in motion as number three got the baton. Experience has shown that numbers one and two may, either accidentally or on purpose, race number three to the finish, hoping to urge his horse to greater speed. Thus the rule enforced by most clubs and Playdays that the last baton carrier must cross the finish line ahead of his teammates or else be no-timed.

The Risks Involved

As mentioned, with three horses and riders running in the arena the chances for mishap are greater in the Baton Relay than in most timed events. Perhaps the biggest danger comes during the baton exchange. Horses new to the contest may be spooked by another racing up from behind and may, as the running horse comes abreast, turn sharply into his path. Horse collisions are dangerous for both horse and rider so care should be taken to use mounts which either have been used in this or similar contests or which demonstrate their calmness under all conditions. Those teams who win in this event consistently are usually those riding stock horses of even temperament, trained for a smooth, fast exchange of the baton. That exchange is usually where the winning team is determined.

This alert young lady is waiting to be "rescued." Notice tracks in dirt from previous contestants. To see how she does, turn the page.

11   THE RESCUE RACE

Where riders like a small amount of acrobatics with their contests, the Rescue Race will give anyone a pretty good workout. As the photos illustrate, the race involves one person on horseback "rescuing" another on foot.

The contest is usually staged in an arena where there is more than 200 feet of clear space, so that a barrel can be set up 180 feet from a starting-finish line. The contestant on horseback races from the starting line, circles the barrel, helps pull the other member of the two-person team up on the horse behind the saddle, then races for the finish line. Both must cross the finish line on horseback.

This can be a timed event or one in which several teams compete at once. Most clubs, posses and riding groups will find it safer—because of the size of conventional arenas—to run it as

Grabbing the saddle and the rider's left arm—and using the horse's momentum—girl member of team swings quickly up as horse circles barrel.

Both contestants get good handholds as horse pivots and prepares to drive for finish line. This is good contest for large clubs or groups where not all participants are mounted.

a timed event. But if space is not a problem, two, three or four teams can run the Rescue Race as a matched contest. Care should be taken to allow plenty of running room between horses since frequently the mounted team member won't be able to hoist his teammate up behind him on the first try—and the horse may be ridden in a circle to try again.

A flag man at the starting-finish line is needed to signal the timers as a team starts and ends its run.

Tips On Technique

The trick of winning in this contest, as you can see, is to get the team member on foot up on horseback the first time the mounted member circles the barrel. It's not as easy as it may look. Several techniques are used by those who run this contest a lot.

The simplest is for the rider to extend his free arm down as he goes into the circle around the barrel. The teammate on foot reaches up to clasp arms, then aided by the horse's movement he swings up on the horse's back as the animal moves in a circle. Some contestants on foot will take a looped rope with them and toss it over the saddle horn as the horse comes abreast of them. With a little assist from the rider, mounting may be easier.

Certainly this requires cooperation between the two members of a team and they need to work out the exact procedure they'll use, and practice it some, before the race. One of the risks in the race is that the contestant on foot will get over-agile as he goes to mount. It's quite possible to swing up **too** vigorously—and go right on over the other side of the horse!

There is no set rule as to which way the rider must circle the barrel or from which side the standing member must be pulled up on the horse.

The Risks Involved

Possibly the most common hazard in the Rescue Race is that the contestant on foot may not quite make it up on the horse in that brief moment when he tries to mount. He may slide down behind the animal and go face down in the dirt or he might even slide under the horse. However, since most contestants who like this contest practice it a good deal beforehand, it is considered a safe race. The few spills that result usually produce more laughs than bruises.

The Rescue Race may also be staged as a two or three-team matched contest, if there is enough arena room. If teams are run singly it is a timed event.

12 THE POTATO RACE

Here's a contest that livens up any day of mounted games! Nearly all contestants like it because The Potato Race is fast, uncomplicated—and the element of luck plays a big part. As the photos show, each contestant rides from the starting line down to the square box containing the potatoes, spears one, then races back to the finish line. It's a timed event—and if you have never played this game you'll be amazed at how elusive those big spuds can be when you're jabbing at them from horseback!

Equipment And Rules

The contest can be run in a pasture or an arena but as with most running games the ground should be disced to give the horses plenty of traction. Mark a starting-finish line across the course and place a square frame, about 24 inches on a side, in the dirt

Approaching the potato-filled box, rider slows his horse. As with flag race, he wants to pause only an instant. Rider who wins this contest is usually the one that spears a spud the first time around the box.

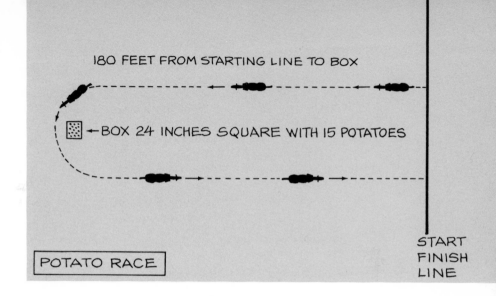

180 FEET FROM STARTING LINE TO BOX

←BOX 24 INCHES SQUARE WITH 15 POTATOES

POTATO RACE

START
FINISH
LINE

Potato Race Pattern

180 feet from the starting line. This frame can be made from 2x4's and should have no bottom. Put 15 good-sized potatoes in the frame. An assistant should stand by to replace a potato each time a contestant spears one. If the number of potatoes doesn't remain the same throughout the contest, it gets progressively harder to spear one from a smaller number.

The spear in this contest should be about five feet long, of wood or light metal construction. The metal point should be straight, about 2½ to 3 inches long. A large nail, taped to or embedded in the spear, does the job quite well.

As each contestant approaches the starting line for the race, an official hands over the spear. Time starts as the contestant's horse reaches the starting line. A flag man should be stationed on the line to signal the timers.

The contestant races to the square frame, circles and spears a potato while going around it. Then he races back to the finish line. The rider must spear the potato without dismounting, must circle the box (in either direction) and must bring the potato back across the finish line on the spear. Once past the finish line, the rider can drop the potato and the spear to the ground. However, if he drops the potato before he gets across the line he must stop and spear the same potato, then finish, in order for his time to count.

A rider is disqualified if his horse steps in the box while going around it.

Tips On Winning

The element of luck enters this contest as far as the rider is concerned when he starts jabbing for a potato. That is why winners in this contest find their horses have to stop and rein well. There is a point as the horse slides to a stop alongside the potato-filled frame when you will have your best chance to spear the spud and take off for the finish line. If you miss this instant your chances of winning in a large field of contestants grows smaller.

Therefore, a good controlled stop on your horse can help win the contest for you. All you need to provide then is good aim with that spear!

Rider holds potato up on spear so it won't slip off on run back to finish line.

13   THE WAGON RACE

In some parts of Texas—notably around Fort Worth and in the Panhandle—the Wagon Race is as popular among adults as among the younger riders. And they play it for keeps too!

The contest has been popular in those areas since 1956 when, it is reported, the Scurry County Sheriffs Posse at Snyder began working out rules. They now vary slightly from one group to another but generally the race, as run by adults, includes the use of protective padding and headgear. The younger contestants sometimes forego that protection.

As the photos indicate, this is a rather spectacular event accompanied by frequent spills—most of them involving overturned wagons. It's obvious, therefore, that it should be run in a large arena with well-turned earth underfoot.

Object of the contest is for one contestant on horseback to pull another in a kid's wagon around a barrel placed 180 feet from the starting-finish line. It is a timed event. The team can circle the barrel to the right or left. The wagon rider must be in the wagon when the race starts and ends and the wagon must be

Football helmet and chest protector are used by some groups that take wagon racing seriously and run it at top speed.

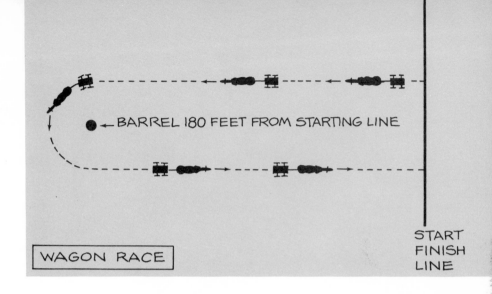

WAGON RACE

Wagon Race Pattern

upright starting and finishing.

Both wagon and rider must circle the barrel. If the rider falls out before getting to the barrel, the wagon rider may run around the barrel, get back aboard and complete the race.

In this race it is not the horse that is flagged but the wagon. Time starts and stops as the wagon crosses the starting-finish line.

Equipment Needed

Most avid wagon racing enthusiasts will put special bracing on whatever wagon they use for this contest. Rules set up by the American Association of Sheriffs Posses and Riding Clubs discourage elaborately-rigged wagons but do authorize a heavier tongue and such underside bracing as may be needed (and it **will** be needed) to stand the strain. Ball-bearing wheels are okay, 10 inches in diameter and two inches thick. The axles should be at least $\frac{1}{2}$ inch in diameter and not more than $\frac{5}{8}$ inch. The axle also should be no longer than to just clear the edges of the wagon so that the wheel is roughly even with the outside of the wagon. There should be no bar or bracing on the wagon for the rider to hold to or to steer with.

The rope used in pulling the wagon should be an ordinary lariat rope tied to the wagon. It may or may not be tied to the wagon tongue. The other end can be tied to the saddle horn but wagon racers almost unanimously urge that it be dallied (looped around the horn) so that the wagon can be disengaged from the horse on a moment's notice.

As mentioned, many wagon riders provide themselves with body protection against spills. A conventional football helmet with face shield will protect the head quite well. Women wagon riders

In action, rider has rope dallied—not tied—to the horn for instant release. He swings wide around barrel so that wagon rider will make a smaller arc and therefore move slower. This

will find a baseball catcher's chest protector good for upper-body protection. Shin guards and knee pads also have been used.

Tips On Technique

Originally, the wagon race was designed as a contest to determine which horse could pull the wagon around the course without the wagon rider taking much of an active role in the proceedings. It was then a disqualification if any part of his body touched the ground. Now, however, the wagon rider can drag one foot and help to balance the wagon during the race as he is

is to keep wagon from whipping out and turning over. Notice wagon rider's foot in the dirt.
It acts as brake and rudder.

able to. The only restriction, by present rules, is that the body
must be clear of the ground crossing the start and finish line.

This means that a good wagon rider can now help a lot to win
the race. It also means that the race is run faster, wagons must
be better braced and contestants better protected than under the
original rules.

The most successful technique in running the course appears
to be the practice of the horseback rider swinging in a fairly wide
circle around the barrel. This has the effect of letting the wagon
turn in a slower, tighter circle with less danger of turning over.

The Risks Involved

The risks in this contest are apparent. The wagon rider can get roughed up in a spill—or in a small arena may come in contact with the arena fence. It is important too that contestants doing the horseback riding dally the rope to the horn rather than actually securing it tightly. A horse can get excited from dragging a wagon behind him and the rider needs to be able to unwind and drop the wagon rope the moment the wagon crosses the finish line.

One other point: Don't run your horse in this contest time after time, for practice. He'll get so shy about a wagon that he'll hate the sight of one. A reasonably good stock horse that reins well will do fine in this event. If anyone has ever roped calves or steers off his back the weight of that wagon won't disturb him. Just don't overdo it.

14 THE KEYHOLE RACE

The Keyhole Race tests the ability of a horse to run in a straight line, stop and roll back. It is a timed event. It requires speed, of course, but it also takes good action and control to win this event.

You run the Keyhole Race in a pattern marked on the ground, usually with white lime. The pattern is in the shape of a big keyhole, with a lane 40 feet long and four feet wide leading to a circle 20 feet in diameter.

Starting from at least 20 feet from the lane entrance, you run your horse up the lane, do a fast rollback inside the circle, then ride back out the lane to the finish line. The entrance of the lane is the starting and finish line. Time is measured as the horse's muzzle crosses the line, going and coming. The contestant is disqualified if his horse steps on the line at any time during the run.

The rider should have good control of his horse as he starts his run.

Line judges are positioned so they can see keyhole pattern from both directions. If horse touches limed area judge will see a puff of white. Photos show riders entering the "keyhole," rolling back and leaving.

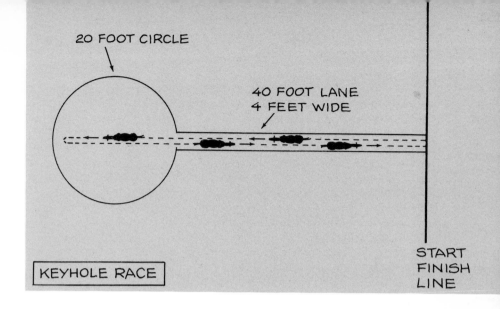

20 FOOT CIRCLE

40 FOOT LANE
4 FEET WIDE

KEYHOLE RACE

START
FINISH
LINE

Keyhole Race Pattern

Judging The Contest

This is a rapidly-run event, ideal for shows where a large number of contestants wish to compete. There is little accident risk involved if it is run in the center of a conventional show or rodeo arena, where the earth is soft.

Using lime as the outline for the keyhole makes it fairly easy to judge since there will be a puff of white whenever a horse's foot strikes a line. Liming equipment is necessary to keep the lines fresh so the judges can do the best possible job.

In addition, some groups use three judges to make sure that all line violations are caught. One judge will stand so he can look up the long axis of the lane and the other two will flank the circle. These judges will usually be on foot.

A flag man, either on foot or on horseback, should signal as the horse enters and leaves the lane, for timing purposes.

Variations

If you don't have any lime-spreading equipment, you may use old tires to shape the keyhole pattern. These are soft enough for horses to step on without injury to their feet. Judges must watch closely, however, since there will not be the same visible evidence of line-crossing as with the lime method.

Do's And Don't's

As in most timed events in an arena, horses will get spooky if they are raced through this pattern too much in practice. One run for warmup purposes is plenty—especially if the horse is familiar with the event. Also, your horse should not be raced into the arena for this event, since he's then apt to be hard to hold motionless before the start of the race.

Training a horse to win in this contest involves little more than the basic training all good stock horses should have. The animal should be taught to rein well—and instantly—and should be worked on smooth rollbacks.

Your horse should run straight too if you want to win the Keyhole Race. The horse that "fishtails" will nearly always hit the line. This is why you need to use that 20 foot start to collect your horse and get him running straight.

And when you can win consistently in the Keyhole Race, you'll *know* you've got a horse with speed and action!

Other publications of the

CORDOVAN CORPORATION

The Texas and Southwestern Horseman

The southwest's monthly Magazine of Western Riding is a lively informative guide to buying, training, enjoying and winning with a western horse. Each month there is news of Quarter Horse, Appaloosa, Pinto and other breed competitions, as well as news of open shows, cuttings, ropings, barrel races and rodeo. Features important "how to" articles by and with the nation's leading stock horse trainers plus tips on horse production and care from outstanding breeders. Subscription: 1 year $3, 2 years $5, 3 years $7.

Training Tips for Western Riders

Trainer-Judge L. N. Sikes and Texas and Southwestern Horseman Editor Bob Gray have filled this inexpensive training manual with horse-country knowhow. There are tips on early colt haltering, bits for young horses, hobbles, barrel racing techniques, cutting lessons and plain talk on training your horse to stop, back and lead properly. Also important suggestions on proper feeding procedures and preparing a horse for halter showing. $3.00

Championship Barrel Racing

The first comprehensive book on the country's exciting new stock saddle sport, written by World Champion Barrel Racer Jane Mayo and Texas and Southwestern Horseman Editor Bob Gray. With action photos, this book tells you essentials of recognizing a good barrel horse, starting a young one, barrel footwork, speed and its control—plus many hauling and contest tips that will help you win more often in competition. $4.00

CORDOVAN CORPORATION

Cypress, Texas   Telephone Houston OV 6-8471